BAIL MONEY
Inspired by actual events

Copyright© 2018 by Tia Hanna

All rights reserved. This book or any portion thereof may not be reproduced without written permission from the publisher or used in any manner whatsoever without the written permission of the author or publisher except for the brief quotations in a review.
Printed in the United States of America
First printing, 2018
ISBN: 978-1-7323399-7-2

SELF-PUBLISHING SERVICES
provided by High Maintenance Publishing & Production, LLC

www.highmaintenance1.com

"Providing Opportunities, Inspiration and Education to Independent Writers."

Author Celeste Celeste
High Maintenance Publishing & Production, CEO

INTRO

I remember watching my mom work at the local Tax Collectors office during the day and cleaning commercial businesses at night with my drunken uncle. During the weekends, I would spend my time pretending to be rich. I watched my mom sweep, mop and vacuum the homes of wealthy people. I would always tell myself that I never wanted to work that hard.

Fast forward to my 23rd year of life. I was a college graduate, a mother to a handsome two-year old boy and a girlfriend/baby-mama to a well-known drug dealer, trying to figure my shit out.

Who would of thought that at the age of twenty-five, I'd own my own bail bonds company? Trust and believe shit was far from easy, but before I get ahead of myself, let me back my ass up and take you to the beginning. Let me tell you how it all started...

CHAPTER 1
2010

"Baby, Mommy is so proud of you, the first in the family to graduate college!" My mom cried as I stood in front of her holding my criminal justice degree. My graduation ceremony had just ended.
"Yeah, you're the first of my baby mama's that even went to college," my baby daddy, Malik, smirked as he handed over our son.
"Thanks asshole," I mumbled.
"Okay, okay Asia and Malik get together so I can take a picture," shouted my mom. "1...2...3..." she snapped the picture.
At that moment, I truly felt proud of myself. Shit ya girl graduated college and was feeling like I had just smoked some weed. I was on cloud ten. Hell, not to mention I was still in a relationship with my son's father and I had just tackled the toughest obstacle I'd faced thus far, graduating college. I can still remember how fulfilled and optimistic for my future I felt in that moment.
Damn was I wrong. Just as I graduated, the economy simultaneously had gone to shit. We had former President Bush to blame for that. No one was interested in hiring an inexperienced college graduate, so shit, I had very limited options. Eventually I came across an ad for a legal assistant in a criminal attorney's office. I was hired for the job, even though I had zero experience, but don't think this was some happily ever type shit. I had the pleasure of working for one of the most arrogant, rude, racist, short, Arab attorneys ever! I mean this motherfucker had the nerve to call me a *dumb ass nigga* at least twice a week. Hell, I was fired over six times in one year because honey I have a mouth too! Call me a 'dumb ass nigga' and I'm calling you a 'dumbass foreign troll', yes, I knew that two wrongs didn't make a right, but shit, you come for me and I'm coming for you, ten times harder. I remember walking into the office one morning, I had just taken a sip of

my French vanilla coffee, feeling good, when in walks Lucifer himself, horns flaring, "See this is why I can't hire niggas, didn't I tell you I needed this stipulation ready before court!" Before I could even utter a word, he slams his office door in my face. Talk about a typical Tuesday. But the worse part was it wasn't even a stipulation that was assigned to me! The shit I had to deal with. I can't say it was all bad because during this time, I met a chick called Lil' Mexico. We developed a friendship that would teach me an important lesson about loyalty, but we'll get into that later.

Around this time, my life was pretty stagnant; work and home was my normal routine, and every now and again I'd go out with my girls. It was Easter night, which was a big deal where I'm from, my crew and I were in crank mode. Webbie was in town and the club was on swole. Lights flashing, smoke coming from the DJ stand, the dance floor felt like it was vibrating from the speakers, and sparkling bottle girls were everywhere, definitely my type of scene. Hair, nails and toes were on point and my Fashion Nova dress had just come in the mail, and honey it hugged every curve on my body.

Me and my bitches were bad, we literally RIP'd the club scene when we stepped in, booty bouncing everywhere. As we made our way to the VIP section. My girl Rhonda bumped me and said "Bitch ain't that Jay over there in the corner?"

Once we made it to the sofa I asked, "Hoe where did you see Jay," I quickly scouted the scene.

"Over there by the bathroom bitch," she shouted back. See Jay used to be my little boo thang back in the day. When I finally laid eyes on him, the nigga was looking as fine as he did back in the day. This man was my white chocolate, thugged out version of Drake. Tattoos covered his body, mouth full of VVS diamonds, hell you might as well say he had a mouth full of money. Not to mention this nigga was dressed head to toe in Versace, all white. Yeah, yeah I know I was with my baby daddy, but I thought, hell, a quick conversation ain't cheating...

I scoped the scene to see if my baby daddy had made it in building yet, but there was no sign of him or his snitching ass

homeboys. *Good,* I thought. With my back arched and titties sitting up nice, I prepared my runway walk. I made my way over to Jay's fine ass. "Damn girl, even after the baby you still look edible." Jay whispered in my ear.
"Boy stop," I giggled. I could smell the Versace cologne he poured on. "So how you been shawty? Still with that family shit?" He asked grabbing my waist with his left hand while running his fingers through my hair with his right. I began to feel weak, and my panties started to get wet.
I responded softly, "Yeah, boo trying to make it work," as I rolled my eyes, "but enough of you asking the questions sweetie. What you been doing? Heard you out of the streets."
"Bail Bonds" he said squeezing my waist.
"Bail bonds? The fuck, don't you gotta be like forty years old to get in the business?" I laughed.
"Hell nawl shawty as a matter of fact since I still have a soft spot in my heart for you I'll put you on." At this point the patron started to kick in and I figured I'd better get his number before I embarrassed myself.
A few days later, I made the call. As I hung up with my white chocolate, I knew my career path was going to be taking a turn for the better, but first, I told the idea of bail bond school to my baby daddy. Of course when I told my baby daddy of the idea, and a brief recap of my conversation with Jay he was excited. "Shit baby mama that's a street nigga legit hustle, you need to go head and go, since that degree of yours isn't being used." It was so typical of him to add an insult in the sentence, I shook my head. I was ready for a change, but it would cost me. Yeah baby daddy claimed to be on board, but that didn't mean he was trying to finance it. Now let me tell you about my baby daddy real quick. He wasn't your average nickel and dime hustler. This nigga was moving major weight, he was the local supplier, had six different foreign cars, a $15,000 Cuban link necklace and every designer shoe. Money was never an issue for him and when it came to our son, but I was excluded from such benefits. But let me give you a quick background before I just throw his ass under the bus, you see by this time we had been together for five years and we had plenty of ups

and downs. When we first met he was like my knight in shining armor, he swept me off my feet with his deep voice. He was like my Denzel Washington, a smooth operator, but was hood like Nino Brown on New Jack City. I mean he took me to Dubai our first-year dating and bought me a BMW 650li, all black. Yeah your girl was living up, I was living lavishly with constant shopping sprees and five star restaurants. No hoe could tell me about my man. But as time went on, so did the honeymoon phase. After I had our first child, shit changed and not for the best, guess the nigga felt like he had me trapped and growing up in a broken home, I didn't want my son to endure the same experience, so I dealt with him cheating on me with thirsty, fake ass, hood rat hoes and the occasional ass whoopings cause I couldn't keep my mouth shut.

So there I was, standing in line at the payday advance store in disgust, listening to this toothless, breath smelling like it just farted, customer complain about how much life sucks and that the world is going to shit. I told myself, *fuck this I'll never allow myself to need anyone ever again*, hoping that this bail bonds thing would be the answer.

September finally came and I was ready to start my two weeks Bail Bonds class in Miami. Bags packed, gas tank on full, I dropped my son off with my mom because I knew Malik would be too busy hustling and hoeing to watch our son, and honey I hit the road.

After passing the test with flying colors and completing a few online courses, I was ready to take on my one-year internship with a well-known bail agency. Jay put me on and this happened to be the same agency where he took his internship and before you knew it my year was up and I had my bail license. I was lit, like a whore in heat; finally it was my time to shine. After watching Jay ball out for a year while I sat back and learned the bail game, your girl was ready to open up! With my own money saved up, I opened up my business and everyone was happy for me, except for one person, my baby daddy. He was feeling salty that I didn't come to him to ask for the money, but shit I felt like since he didn't want to help with

school, why help now and try to take credit. Naw boo, I wanted to do it on my own to show his ass and I did.
In August of 2012, the doors opened to Around the Clock Bail Bonds, your girl was 'glowed up.' I turned a dream into reality, a 1200 square foot office, flat screens mounted on damn near every wall, marble flooring that sparkled when the sun hit, and a leather black sectional that was specialty ordered from Cali. Shit I amazed myself and word spread fast on my opening and how the office was dope as hell. Shit started to pop quickly, it seemed like every dope boy and booster were going to jail and calling ya girl. "Lik's girl will help bond out anyone with enough money down," the streets were talking, damn. In the first month I profited $5,500! I was straight hustling. Once my name started poppin, the uninvited attention from niggas and hating ass bail bond agents followed. Bail Agents started talking shit about my alleged "ghetto ways" in an effort to divert attention back to their bail agencies. They'd been struggling for business since I stepped on the scene, but that shit ain't work, some real weak type shit. Niggas started disrespecting the game too, jumping in my inbox trying to holla at me. My baby daddy wasn't feeling it at all but guess who he was mad with…me.
"The fuck you so friendly for?" Malik asked one late night at the office as I came in from posting yet another bond, feeling myself.
"Huh?" I asked in a confused voice as I sat down at my desk, putting together a client's file.
"Bitch, listen don't fucking disrespect me, I'm a real ass nigga and playing stupid will get your white ass fucked up," he screamed as he made his way towards me.
"Malik, come on, I wouldn't" I cried out. I knew this wasn't going to end good. The next thing I knew he grabbed the back of my hair and slung me down to the carpet. As I tried to get up, he stomped his size twelve foot into my back. He then drug me by my hair across the carpet, into the front office where my phone sat on the desk, my knees were on fire.
"Since you wanna open Facebook messages from these bum ass niggas, tell them fuck boys to buy you a new phone," he

yelled, spit coming from his mouth. He slammed the phone into the side of my face. Once he realized he had only cracked the screen, he slammed it on the ground, shattering it.
I fell to the floor with a bruised back, a patch of hair torn from my head, a busted lip, and a black eye. I cried hysterically, I was in shock and disbelief. Tears were streaming down my face uncontrollably, but my baby daddy just looked at me and before he walked out he turned and calmly said, "Fuck you crying for white girl, you caused this, hurry up and get up and take ya ass home."
Although this wasn't the first time my baby daddy had put his hands on me, this time was different. I thought I was someone, and most of all I thought I was the complete woman to him. I had my own business, own car, own money and I always made sure our son was good, without having to ask him for anything anymore. I thought to myself what else could he ask for, but that moment only reminded me that the power I thought I had, was only a figment of my imagination that the same respect he had for me before was the same respect he had for me now... none.
Hurt physically and mentally, I picked myself up and made my way to the car. It was cold as shit. I felt like my legs were paralyzed. All I could think was that one day I was going to have to leave his ass, but that wasn't in the deck of cards for me yet, little did I know I would be getting another surprise.

It was December, four months since the opening of my company, Around the Clock Bail Bonds and my period was late. I finally got up from the bed and tip-toed into the bathroom, not wanting to wake anyone. "Damn, Tia just pee on the fucking stick," I said aloud to myself. I sat for three minutes on the toilet waiting for the results, and then my fear came true. The positive sign was as clear as day. I stood up, staring at myself in the mirror as I laid the stick on the counter, in disbelief because I was on birth control. Then, to make the moment worst, in walks Malik, for his morning routine.

"What's wrong?" he yelled shaking the last bit of pee from his penis, but before I could utter the words, *I'm pregnant*, he beat me to it, "Damn boo boo we having another Lik Lik," he said. Looks like he was excited, unfortunately the feeling was not mutual, talk about an early fucking Christmas present.
Now I know what you're thinking. How could you have another baby from a nigga you wanted to get away from? The way I saw it, I was financially able to support another child, plus I always wanted my kids to have the same father. One sperm donor was enough for me.
Not to mention Malik and I planned to have more kids, and although the thought of another abortion came to mind, I decided to go through with this pregnancy. Hell after all I still loved him.

4:30 a.m. on September 6, 2013 was my check in time at Health Park Children's Hospital. Malik, my mom, and I made our way to the birthing section and into the room assigned to me. This was definitely an exciting time for me and my baby daddy, a time when I forgot all the bullshit we went through. I was happy to share this moment with him because he wasn't there for our first son's delivery. Don't think that I didn't appreciate my mother's presence, but one thing about my mom is she'd be with me right or wrong.
Around 10:30 a.m. my contractions started and my bitch mode was in full effect. I cussed out my baby daddy, I'm sure I called him every cuss word in the directory, I even made up a word "assbitchfuck."

1:17 p.m. rolls around and I finally received the epidural, then I received the type of news, that would scare any parent. My baby boy was breached, the umbilical cord was wrapped around his precious little neck and an emergency c-section would have to be done. Tears and emotions took over as I was wheeled quickly away and into the surgery room.
Moments later the procedure was underway and right by my side I had my baby daddy. He had a look of horror on his face as he glimpsed over to watch the doctor remove our son from

my stomach. After what seemed like forever, our daughter was finally held in the air and next thing you know my baby daddy released my hand and passed out. *What a little bitch*, I thought to myself, all this shit he's always talking but can't take the sight of a little open wound, which happened to be my stomach with my liver and gallbladder removed and then put back into place. I laughed to myself. None of that mattered, all that did was my ten-pound and two-ounce baby boy was healthy. He made it through a rough nine months, the gun play, the fire bombs and all the sleepless nights. Did I skip that part? Let me back up…

CHAPTER 2

It was 6:42 a.m., Saturday morning and the sun was glaring directly in my eyes. Trying to block the sun with my hand, I rolled over to get off the bed to go pee. *Beep Beep* my phone notifications were going off, eleven missed calls. *FUCK!* I thought to myself, damn all baby daddy's calls. *The hell does he want,* I thought as I rubbed my pregnant belly. I sighed as I sat on the toilet, it felt like I was peeing at least fifteen times a day.
My cell phone went off as I wiped my freshly shaved cat, it was baby daddy again, "Baby get the fuck up, some bullshit happened at the office, looks like someone shot this shit up, hurry up cause the crackers are here and I'm gonna dip. You know I ain't on no interaction with them," he yelled. My heart felt like it stopped in that very moment, I zoned out, then I shook my head, realizing this nigga just hung up the phone on me, "The fuck, oh my God," I screamed to myself as I rustled around for some pants, *Who the fuck, what the fuck, why the fuck,* were the questions popping in my head. "Damn bro, baby daddy ain't beefin with no niggas and shit I get motherfuckers out of jail, so I know a bitch ain't mad with me?" I said out loud. My head was spinning and my adrenaline was pumping, like the first time me and my baby daddy popped Molly. Before I knew it I was doing the dash and had to just start calming myself down, breathing in and out, telling myself *it's gonna be ok, it's gonna be ok.*
When I finally pulled into the plaza parking lot, my shit was roped off like it was a First 48 crime scene, yellow tape around the parking lot in front of my office, shell casings shattered all across the black pavement. I was in disbelief, I closed my eyes, wanting this bullshit to be a dream, but when I opened my eyes, shit was still there. "Ma'am," the officer said as he knocked on my passenger window. I didn't respond, "Ma'am," he said again, this time with a little force behind his voice, looking at him, I rolled down my window. "You the

owner of this establishment, I shook my head yes and put my car in park.

I opened my door and stepped out, shook by the sight that was before my eyes, glass shattered everywhere, bullet holes in the wall and a few hit the TV mounted in the waiting room wall. I mean there was so much glass that some homeless guy stepped on it from the other side of the plaza. As I looked around, my eye caught a particular vehicle driving by, as the officer began asking questions, "Ma'am, do you know who would try to cause harm to you or your business?" Ignoring his ass, I watched as the driver side window of the black Mercedes rolled down and to no surprise, it was Jay, he smiled, nodded, and shot a peace sign at me. I mean *this bitch nigga was fucking laughing at me.* At that moment I knew this punk bitch had something to do with this.

"Ma'am, are you ok?" The little fake Doogie Houser looking ass officer asked.

"No," I snapped back and now diverting my attention back to my office, I responded, "No officer, I have no idea, I'm just a female in the business world." You see my man was from the streets and always used to tell me, never be a snitch, no matter what the situation is or how you fell, never be a snitch, so call me dumb but I was sticking to the G-Code.

By this time, the word was out about the shooting at my office, it seemed like the whole city was doing drive-by's, being nosey as fuck. I mean so called friends came up there, asking questions, but shit like I told the officer, I ain't know who the hell shot it up. As the anger subsided, sadness came over me as I began to sweep the glass from my office; my mom had finally showed up with tears rolling down her rosy cheeks. She walked into the office with her blonde hair in a ponytail, "Asia, baby are you ok?" she cried out.

"Yeah mom, I mean what can I say, this shit is crazy," trying to hold back tears. See you have to understand, I don't cuss ever at my mom, but she was my best friend and that's the type of relationship we had. A best friend and a motherly one as well, but right now we both knew I didn't need a mother, I

needed a friend to talk to. "Mom I guess I pissed the right person off, huh?" I snickered
"Really Asia?" my mom smiled back. I couldn't bring myself to tell her that I knew the nigga behind this, you know some things are worth keeping to yourself.
"Oh my God, Asia are you ok?" A familiar voice asked and as I turned around, I seen my home girl Lil Mexico lifting the yellow tape up, telling the officer that she works here, after confirming that she was telling the truth, the officer allowed her to come in. "This shit roped off like it's a murder scene," she smirked as the local TV station van pulled up. "But really what the fuck bitch, this got something to do with Malik? That bastard better not have brought his shit over to your office," Lil Mexico demanded to know.
"Man boo, I already know who did it, the jerk drove by to let me know it was him, but I ain't saying shit to the police," and then I whispered in her ear, "Jay did it and I know for sure cause I seen his lil worker in the camera footage, watch." I pulled out my phone and replayed the shooting and in plain sight, there he was Lil Buddy, the trigger happy seventeen-year-old nigga from the old projects and Jay's right hand man. I grinned and told Lil Mexico, "Told the police the cameras aren't working and that their getting maintenance. Finally!" I yelled as the glass company arrived. Six hours later, after sweeping, mopping, plastering bullet holes and a fresh glass installation the office was back to normal. I even got a new TV to replace the fucked up one. Lil Mexico, my mama, Tony (which was a buddy my baby daddy sent over) and I were exhausted but excited to have the office back to normal. With the new LED 'OPEN' sign my baby daddy brought, shit one monkey ain't stop no show and your chick was back to business. Four months pregnant, hormonal, emotional and now having to deal with this punk bitch Jay.
Months had passed and although baby daddy had some retaliation thoughts in his mind, he was dealing with his own enemy, the Feds and the conspiracy charge he was facing. Not to mention he couldn't even move how he wanted because he had a GPS ankle monitor attached to him, so he was fucked in

more ways than one and that shit made the living conditions a little rocky, but the bail bond company was still blossoming. It seemed like the shooting Jay put out on my business did the opposite of what he thought. Instead of people bonding back out through him shit everyone was feeling like my office was popping and people wanted to be a part of that. Crazy I used to think *these people really fuckin with me because of some hatin' ass drama, well damn, guess I can't be mad, nigga I'm the winning team.*

At nine months pregnant, I was feeling fat and dealing with swollen ankles, and damn near looking like three hundred pounds. My ankles were as big as a damn bowling ball, but my mom insisted on a baby shower and the shit was over the top. I mean this lady had a chocolate fountain, balloons and flowers galore, white doves, picture booth, a DJ, a professional photographer, red carpet and some damn belly dancers performing, shit was crazy, but it was beautiful and it was so extra, but extra was what my mom did, and where I got it from.

This time baby daddy was even acting right, not sure if it had anything to do with his curfew or the GPS monitor, but fuck it, it didn't matter because he was pampering the hell out of me, giving my daily foot massages, getting my nails done every three weeks, and sending me to the hair dresser every two weeks. Life was good, no bullshit, money climbing, and getting all of my baby daddy's attention, shit was great.

But in my world good things, didn't last long.

It was Tuesday night and I just tucked my son into bed and made my way to the bedroom where Malik was waiting for me to watch the show, American Greed. Twenty minutes had passed, as we laid there, both of us started to rub my belly as our princess was kicked. My cell phone rung and the caller ID read, *anonymous*. Now usually shit like that is suspect to me, but my instinct told me to answer. It wasn't till after that I wish I hadn't. "Ms. Mines?" politely asked the woman on the other line.

Hesitantly I answered, "Yes" trying to figure out it this damn woman was a bill collector or a mother nervous trying to bond out her child.
"This is Sargent Stapple with the police department. Your office has been vandalized with bullet holes," she firmly announced. All I could do was shake my fucking head and glare at Malik.
"Ok I'll be right there."
"I fucking knew it, Lik," I yelled, "I knew once I posted Harpo's $250,000 bond, that bitch nigga Jay was gonna have a problem with it." Frustrated, but not surprised because I knew Jay was thirty-eight hot cause he was trying to post bond for the same client as me. He was blowing up his baby mama line but shit the nigga's mama came through and dropped off the twenty-five bands to me, so it wasn't my fault he was blowing up the wrong mama's phone. So hell I took the chance and did what any other bail bondsman would do, post that shit and collect that money and make that bank deposit. *Fuck it* I reassured myself, *ain't nothing but some pocket change* I snickered.
This time when I pulled up to my office in my recently purchased red 750li BMW, my belly slightly bursting through my sundress, I held my head high, confidence level thru the roof, I wasn't even phased by yet another bitch move directed towards me.
"Well ma'am, here we are again," the detective stated as he walked towards me, "So are you going to finally admit to us that Jay is responsible for this, Ms. Mines," he asked arrogantly. I pretended to ignore the question, although inside of my head I was trying to the figure out how he knew.
I played it cool. "Who?" I snapped back.
"No need to get defensive with me, you don't think the streets talk?" He whipped back.
"Well damn, detective looks like you got your work cut out for yourself, now don't you? Look at my current situation, I'm eight months pregnant, with a shot up office. Don't you think if I knew who was responsible, I would tell you?" I walked

away from the detective before giving him a chance to respond.

The detective rolled his big, bugged-out blue eyes and told the other officers, "Just make a report, she's not cooperating." Fuck a damn report, dumbass I could feel anger emerge as I walked into my once again-shot up office. I check my watch for the time, fucking 1:00 in the damn morning. The police cars began to pull off and I watched as lights faded in the morning mist. The streets were quiet, with an occasional car ridin' by.

Sitting in Lil Mexico's office chair, rubbing my belly, my daughter kicked vigorously. I attempted to figure out where to start and who to call. Suddenly phone my went off; it was baby daddy. "What's up hun," I sighed.

"What are you doing baby, is it bad? You want me to come there? The crackers gone?" He questioned with a concerned tone.

"I'm good boo, and you don't have to come I'll handle it, and yeah the police are gone. I'll call you later and keep you updated." I just wanted to get off the phone. I mean, did I really want my son to be disturbed because his mommy's office was shot up? Nigga thinks he has all the game, he knew my ass would say no.

It was time to call the landlord I said to myself, knowing damn well I didn't want to, but hell I needed this shit cleaned up and my dumbass never got the glass people's number when they came last time. "God dammit," yawned Steve. "Screw those damn haters! Let me get the hell on up and call the emergency line for the glass people, I'll be up there shortly," he instructed. "You're the best Steve, see you soon," I said with an enthusiastic voice, not ready to make this second call to my mom.

"Hello, Asia is everything is ok," my mom quietly whispered in the phone.

I couldn't hold back, I cried out, "Mom he did it again and I just feel like giving up right now." Feeling defeated, tears rolled down my face and my eyes started to puff up. Snot began to stream drizzle out of my nose, I hung up the phone and yelled with all my might, "FUCK," realizing this bastard put another hit on my office, pissed off and fed up. I started to dial a number I told myself I'd never dial ever again.

"Fuck you want, since you ain't block the number bitch," the voice demanded.

"You already know Jay, the hell you beefing with a pregnant chick for? Ain't enough niggas in the streets for that?" I asked calmly, trying to hold back the name I wanted to call him.

"When the fuck is this going to end? After everything between us, please stop," I pleaded desperately.

"Close shop hoe." and the phone hung up.

Livid, heart racing rapidly, emotions high, my baby girl feeling like she's ready to rip though my pussy walls, my adrenaline was pumping in my veins. I went into beast mode. *Six more weeks,* I said to myself, *then I can rest.* By the time Steve and the glass people arrived, vacuums were going and trash bags were full, I was damn near done, the weather was sixty-five degrees and I was sweating. Shit as the glass was being replaced, your girl was on the website, all I could think was *Bitch make all the money, fuck how anyone feels, I'm not going to sleep any time soon.* I told my landlord with a Kool-Aid grin on my face, "They are gonna have to come harder than this to get me to go out of business."

"That's the spirit," he smiled back.

By seven a.m., you didn't even know my office was shot at, windows back up, bullet holes covered, carpet vacuumed and I was exhausted, ready for a hot bath and bed. Oh let me not forget that mom brought her ass up there around three in the morning and helped with bringing the office back to normal. It was time for me to go home and I never received not one call about any shooting at my office, hell the fucking news people didn't even give a damn.

Finally, I arrive home, where Malik had our son dressed and breakfast made for me, "Wow," I smiled, looking at the pancakes, bacon and eggs.

"Asia, baby I got you a massage for later, enjoy your breakfast. I'm taking little man to my mom so you got the house to yourself baby, relax." he smiled with all his gold fronts shining back at me. He and my son walked out the front door after they finished breakfast.

I took a relaxing shower and applied lotion all down my body. I hopped in bed and ate the breakfast baby daddy made, Speaking softly to my unborn child, rubbing my oversized belly, "Baby, I know you've been strong for the both of us, I love you. Just keep holding on, your time for arrival is close."

A few days passed since the unspoken incident at my office occurred and Malik suggested having his homeboy sit at the office overnight since the bullshit was happening after hours and although I wasn't completely sold on the idea, but shit what other choice did I have? Fuck it I gave in hoping that having his boy up there would prevent anything else from happening.

July 1st, two weeks from my due date, the excitement of our baby girl's arrival had the house in excitement, bonds were getting posted, I was constantly shopping for our little girl and our little prince. Everything seemed to be in order and most of all no bullshit was happening, guess Malik's idea worked.

But I guessed wrong.

July 12th, 2013, 2:43a.m., that infamous phone call came through. Rolling over, drool out the side of my mouth, I glanced at my phone. The caller ID read *Office*. "What the hell does Ray Ray want?" I whined "Hello," wiping the sleep out of my eyes.

"Asia, Asia someone just threw a fire bomb at the windows," panic in his voice. "The police and fire crew are on their way, shit I can't believe it but the glass didn't even break!" I suddenly heard the sirens from the fire truck and police cars.

"Ray Ray are you ok?" I asked calmly, allowing him to take a second to breathe.

"Yeah boss lady I'm good. Shit I know you have to check into the hospital this morning, you good? I got this Asia, no worries," he said, and we hung up.

At that moment I turned on my back and looked up at the wall, just laying there next to Malik who was snoring loud as hell and just said to myself *princess is almost here and boy I couldn't wait because that fuck nigga Jay ain't seen shit, the bitch is coming back with a vengeance.* I smiled, rested my eyes and fell back asleep, only to wake up to my alarm clock. It was time to give birth to my little solider.

CHAPTER 3

I had a new baby and soon, I'd be moving into my new office location. Malik and I decided that a change would be a welcomed adjustment to my business. With all the bullshit that had taken place in the last year, I was slowly gaining popularity, but for being "ghetto" and "dangerous." *Shit why not move into a more suburban area,* I thought. Finding the new location wasn't hard, especially since it was only one town over, nothing major, cause ya girl was only a skip hop away from the jail, plus I made our den at home my own little personal office. What was more exciting was the fact that my boo, Malik had stuck both hands in his pockets for the new office location, which meant money saved in my bank account and more head for him.

Life was going good, but Malik had acquired a few legal issues while setting up the new office. He was being charged with conspiracy and trafficking, so shit was looking crazy for him. I mean the nigga had spent over $60k in lawyer fees, only to be looking at jail time in the end. With that shit looming over his head and how deep he dug in his pockets for the new office, I knew I'd have to step my game up because Malik had to take several seats until his case was over.

Six months had passed and the new location was doing numbers like it was supposed to and our family, despite the legal shit was doing good, even Malik was stepping up as a father. He was helping with more hands-on type shit, instead of just reaching into his pockets all the fucking time when it had something to do with the kids. Hell, on top all of that, this nigga did a whole 360 in the bedroom, spicing shit up. I guess he figured if he had to go lay down for a while, fucking me crazy, would keep my pussy in check till he came home.

Oil massages, foot rubs and his debut with starburst all made its way into our bedroom and in the sheets. *Yeah, I know starburst right? But ladies I swear something about the starbursts, will make a nigga eat the hell out of your pussy, I mean my baby daddy literally sucked the soul out of me. This nigga sucked so good he had me booking us a vacation to the Dominican Republic, and I paid for everything!* That summer I booked first class flights and rented a penthouse, we were loving each other like when we first met, butterflies in my stomach and shit. Before we made our way back to the states, we got each other's names tatted on our chest, we were on some poetic justice type shit. It was us against the world; fuck what anyone thought.

A year passed and it was our baby girl's birthday party at the local yacht club and the scene looked like a mini Wizard of Oz, with pony rides and people walking around dressed up as lions and shit and a chick that looked just like Dorothy. Our daughter had presents by the boatload; big, small, colorful ass boxes were under and on top of the gift table. She was getting spoiled by everyone. I even received an unwanted gift during her birthday party when some ratchet chick made her cottage cheese ass way into my presence. The type of bitch whose rent was equivalent to a pedicure. I stood there with a confused ass look. What could we possibly have in common? Why the fuck and who the fuck invited you, type stare. "You don't know me Asia, but I should introduce myself, I'm Nika and I'm three months pregnant with Malik's baby. Since he don't wanna tell you, I will," she proudly stated, with a punk looking ass smirk on her face.

Fucking stupid bitch, who the fuck you take me for coming to my fucking daughter's birthday. I should beat your $2 Old Navy flip flop wearin ass, cheap, stiff ass weave, mutt lookin ass. I screamed in my head. On the outside I kept my composure. I seen bitches low-key lurking in the cut waiting for my reaction. I swiftly scanned the room for Malik hoe ass, but with him nowhere in sight, I snickered and responded. "Listen here boo boo kitty, you think you did something by coming here and making up shit, dumbass, in front of Malik and my friends and family. Everyone knows that I'm Lik's always and forever and you were, if anything, a three in the morning suck and fuck and keep it pushing. You are pathetic and if you were pregnant by MY MAN, then why the fuck he got you looking the way you do with that stiff ass weave?" I laughed devilishly as I turned my back and walked off, leaving the joke ass hoe where she stood.

It was a struggle trying to walk confidently and stress free while thirty-eight hot and beyond livid, ready to grab my Glock and beat the shit outta Malik. I finally found that piece of shit and gracefully grabbed his arm under mine. I shot a smile at our guests and excused him from his homeboys. I walked him into the family restroom, quickly locking the door behind us and glared into Malik's eyes. I was trying to refrain from punching him in the eye, he smiled and asked, "Baby what's up, why you got that Asia look?"

Feeling the steam coming from my ears, I yelled, "Who the fuck is Nika and why did this hoe just come step to me at my own daughter's birthday hollering she fucking pregnant, from your lil dick ass?"

"What the fuck do you mean? Fuck you always listening to bitches anyways," he snapped back at me, as though the shoe was on the other foot like it was my fault or something for stepping to his sorry ass about the bitch. Then to add insult to injury he added, "You let a no name ass hoe come tell you anything and now you look like a fucking dumbass, cause the shit ain't motherfucking true."

Malik grabbed the door handle, unlocked the door and quickly walked out, leaving me standing there, staring into the bathroom mirror, tears streaming down my eyes, feeling lost, sad, embarrassed. My heart literally felt like it stopped in that moment. I couldn't believe just when everything was going good, here came the bullshit. I turned the water faucet on and splashed my face. Grabbing the paper towel from the rack I wiped my face to remove the smeared mascara, then I grabbed my 3-D mascara tube from my back pocket and reapplied the mascara on my reddish eyes. I quickly pulled myself together; repositioning my titties, adjusted my high-waisted jeans, ran my fingers through my hair, and touched up my lace front. I opened the bathroom door and walked out that bathroom, leaving a piece of my heart in that spot. I took a deep breath and walked out with my head high, people looked on, but no one approached me about the situation, not even my mother.

The party went on and Malik and I blew out candles with our baby girl and smiled for the camera.
They say when it rains it pours and it was pouring down on my relationship. Since the day of our baby girl's party, the tension was so thick in our household you'd have to drill to get through it. Constant arguing, name calling and a few physical altercations, shit was bad, hell during that time we didn't even sleep in the same bed. Then, to add to the frustration, Malik lost trial and had to pay another $45k to his attorney to entice the prosecution. Ultimately, he received a 'light' sentence, per the judge who gave him eighteen months in Federal Custody, two years house arrest and thirty-six months of probation. Next thing you know Malik was sent off while the kids and I were left alone.
But one monkey doesn't stop the show, so I regained focus back into my business and got my mojo back. My hustle game was stronger than ever, not to mention the phones were ringing off the hook. It was like Drakes' *Hotline Bling*. Everyone needed to post bail and wanted to go through me. Word was spreading like wild fire about that bum bitch Nika and the birth of her son. I know everyone was trying to peep me and how I felt about everything, but I didn't care. *If it ain't about no money a bitch better not call my phone* I told myself, *fuck that bitch and her baby, that ain't got shit to do with me and mines.* With Malik locked up, I wasn't stuntin' a damn thing but owning some shit, getting assets like the white rich people, fuck clothes and cars I wanted big shit, and I had my eyes set on a few upscale residential properties, hoping to cop one to make my home. I figured why rent a mini mansion when I can own one instead.
Eighteen months passed quickly and Malik was finally released and although the kids were beyond excited to see him, because Malik refused to have his kids visit him in prison, the only way they saw him was this skype type shit he had set up. This was the first time in eighteen months that they could actually hug their daddy. I was thrilled but only a little, with the distance and this unknown circumstance regarding this baby, there was a definitely a void in our relationship.

That void really made itself present when I introduced him to the idea of buying a house. "What the fuck you rushing for? A nigga just got out!" he exclaimed in frustration.

"The market is going to go back up so nigga time isn't on our side, as it hasn't been for the past 18 months and it's an investment for this family," I snapped back. Shit I guess he was feeling bitter since he found out that the bitch's baby was actually his, so hearing about $30,000 closing costs and shit wasn't his cup of tea. "Nigga I held this fucking family down while you been gone, sending you $1,000 every other week and handling all financial affairs by myself, not even fucking with your money and you catching attitudes about helping this family get a fucking house?" I hollered in disappointment, "Not to fucking mention you had a damn baby on me and I still stayed here by your side, faithfully. Man ok."

"Fuck you, that's what you're supposed to do, as my damn woman! You pay the fucking the closing costs and whatever the fuck else needs to be paid, since you want this house." he clapped back.

"Cool, I know how to handle this," I sarcastically responded, as we sat on the opposite side of our black and gold custom leather couch, listening to the damn beeping noise of his ankle monitor go off every fifteen seconds. We both sat there in silence and it was in that moment I had an epiphany. From the times I got my ass whooped, the mental abuse of not being good enough, to now dealing with a whole baby from another bitch and this motherfucker has the nerve to catch a fucking attitude with me, after I continued to stay with his ass as if we were married, going through the thick and thin. I thought to myself, *Man, fuck this shit, I'm a bad ass bitch; a business owner. I mean I'm like 21 Savage, "I got 1,2,3,4,5,6,7,8 M's in my bank account," I don't have to deal with this nigga and his shit.*

The next morning on my Cardi B shit, I hopped in my Benz Coupe, hauled ass down to the bank and got a cashier's check for $32,623.58. I called my real estate agent and confirmed that we would be meeting the broker to sign the papers and give the check for the closing costs as previously negotiated.

Four hours later, I walked out the broker's office with a set of keys, a garage door opener and an added title to my name, 'homeowner.' I did it all on my own. I mean I literally was on cloud nine that day, I had the biggest smile on my face, like the damn Kool-Aid man and I mean nothing could get in my way. I had just closed on a six-bedroom, five-bathroom, three-story home! It was me against the world and that meant Malik too. I came back to the house, Malik was gone to probation and I packed me and the kids' belongings and hauled ass to my mom's house, but not before I left a note for Malik:

After nine years of loving you and bringing two amazing children into this world, I'm done. I cannot forgive you this time for your fuck up, this baby will never be accepted so therefore I can't be with you. I love you Malik but I love me more and I will always be a shoulder for you to cry on just not a shoulder you can sleep with anymore. I hope you accept this for what it is and let me go peacefully.

Always and forever,
Asia

After finally calling it quits, I was waiting for renovations to be completed in my home, the kids and I moved into my mom's waterfront condo. A few days after leaving the house, Malik finally called me, as I figured he would and calmly said, "Bitch I made you, you think it's that sweet, that you gone buy a house in Coconut Pointe and think I won't know where you live and you just move on after all these years? You're dumber than I fucking thought, see you soon." And he hung up. All I could was shake my head. I knew that there would repercussions for leaving him because he always made it clear that breaking up would never be an option for me and he would make that known to me as time followed.
Finally, three months after signing on the dotted line, my home was ready. The renovations were complete and it was move in time! With the movers and my mom supervising the placement of the furniture everything was going as scheduled.

Hair pulled back, in my cut-up shorts and sports bra I was unpacking my car filled with clothes from my mom's house when an unfamiliar car slowly drove up and stopped behind my car. Unsure if it was Malik, fear rushed over my body as I tried to look into the dark tinted windows and what seemed like forever the driver window finally let down and a redbone nigga stuck his arm out. Relieved it wasn't Malik, I asked "Can I help you?" in a defensive voice.

"Damn shawty I ain't from here but goddamn I need to be," he confidently said. The redbone nigga opened up the car door and stepped out. Looking like Nelly, tall, light-skinned, mouth full of gold with two chains hanging from his neck, rocking the new Balenciaga shoes, his ass was clean from head to toe. "Ummm ok, do I know you?" I asked with a smile.

"No but you need to, shit I ain't from here I was just visiting my partner, a nigga stay in Palm Beach, but for you I'll make that drive everyday if I need to." he said back. I mean the nigga was smooth, as he bit down on his bottom lip and surveyed my body from head to toe with his baby eyes, rubbing his goatee.

"Oh really?" I flirted back, now my defense was down and a smile slowly grew across my face.

"Hell yeah baby, I see you busy moving in and shit and a nigga would love to help, but I got business to attend on the road," his swung arms around and I got a glimpse of his Rolex watch he had on, "but I would love to chat it up on the phone with ya." he smiled.

Still a little hesitant because although Malik and I were newly broken up. I still wasn't ready to move on but then that little person on my shoulder said, "Girl fuck that use this nigga as a distraction. He ain't no broke nigga, shit he's driving a Porsche Cheyenne and it ain't no rental, bitch do ya thing!"

We exchanged numbers and moments after he drove off, my cell phone notifications went off and it was a text, 'You're so damn fine, I forgot to get your name, but I'm Rico and baby I'm gonna make you my lady. Hit this line when you're settled into your home.' Boy when I tell you Rico was a distraction, he damn sure was.

CHAPTER 4

Three months after we met, Rico took me to Jamaica for a baecation, especially since all the stress I've been having to put up with Malik and his anger towards me since I broke up with him. *I mean one minute this nigga is cool as a cooler and the next ready to go to war with me, like I stole a brick of cocaine from him.* I needed this baecation to escape his wrath, first class flight, all the alcohol I could consume, while traveling to the beautiful beaches of Montego Bay. Sparkling deep blue ocean and me running in the water in my thong bikini, letting my ass hang out and giggle was the perfect view for anyone especially Rico. Of course, he loved watching me tease him, as I wrestled with the ocean waves on the beaches of Jamaica. Tipsy as the margaritas kicked in, stumbling back to the lounge chair where Rico sat back and laughed at me. "Baby are you ok, want to go lay down," he gently asked, as I drunkenly smiled at him. I mean this nigga was so concerned about me and that's what I adored about him, always concerned with my needs and wants, making sure they are always met, no lie this nigga had my mind blown. So opposite of the "tough love" shit Malik was on, although he had his passionate moments. Rico was gentle and kind all the time, it's like he could read my mind.

His hands caressing my curvy body as he rubbed sunblock all over my fat ass under the bright, beautiful sun rays of Montego Bay Beach. "Damn baby, I love you, I love everything about you," Rico whispered in my ear. I was always taught to not be a "sucker" for a man, like I did for Malik, I couldn't help but to eat up the words Rico fed me. I mean he was everything I could ask for handsome, funny, freaky in the bedroom and breaded up, Rico owned several trucking companies dealing with imports and exports, internationally and his personal assets were no joke. This nigga owned a condo on South Beach, timeshares in the Hamptons and a gorgeous fifteen-bedroom mansion in Atlanta. Not to mention all six of his vehicles were paid for

cash; Rolls Royce, Bentley, Range Rover, Maybach, Porsche 911 and an Ashton Martin. This nigga was no joke and with him spoiling me every chance he got, my thoughts of reconciliation with Malik slowly faded away. One weekend, Rico spent a cool $15,000 on me at Neiman Marcus.
But with all the bragging and trips every weekend, Malik began to get wind of all of our excursions and wasn't at all happy about it, instead that nigga went into a rage lashing out through text messages. He ranged from "Fuck you whore" to "Stupid bitch" to even sending one of his "workers" to shoot up my Maserati Gran Turismo which was parked at my office over the weekend. Malik had really gone off the grind and no one could control him. I even reached out to his uncle to talk some sense in this nigga, but no one could get him to chill out. I was just glad that all of this craziness from Malik didn't drive Rico away, shit it actually made him go harder. It was like he used Malik's actions as a challenge. "Baby that nigga can't drive me away from you, I just want to make sure you and your kids are safe, I wanna be your protector," Rico stated to me as he stared into my eyes. We sat in the Autobody Collision and Paint Shop waiting to pick up my car from the repairs from the bullets. "Whatever he does, I'll fix and outta respect with that nigga being your baby daddy and all, I ain't gonna put my hands on his ass either." as he swiped his American Express Black Card for $7,500 and we walked out. Rico hopped into his Bentley and me into my Maserati.
But when I drove away with Rico following closely behind, I couldn't help but tear up with the thoughts of Malik and I beefing. Don't get me wrong, I loved Rico, but I never wanted me and Lik to end up like this. I never wanted to hurt Malik. I just didn't want a relationship with him, but with him showing out the way he is, I couldn't help but to want to reach out to him and to try to mend things between us. After all he's the father to my two wonderful children and with things the way they were the kids hadn't seen their father in weeks. So once I made it home and Rico took off to Miami to handle his business, I reached out to Malik. "Hey can we talk?"

"What the hell you want Asia, want to humiliate me more with your fuck toy and Instagram posts?!?" Malik yelled back into the phone.

"No, I'm just trying to speak to you and let you know the kids miss you and I do too. I don't wanna fight with you baby daddy." I pleaded on the phone. What seemed like forever was an awkward moment of silence, then I could hear a faint cry. Malik responded, "I just want my family back," and in that moment my heart felt weak and a sense of vulnerability came across. I was head over heels for Rico, but Malik always held a part of my heart and when he invited himself over to the house to see the kids and I, I couldn't resist. This is what started the roller coaster ride between Rico, Malik and I. Let's be honest I was fucking both niggas and yeah I know that sounds like some hoe shit, but I was conflicted between the two, so I played the game, hell I had my cake and ice cream too. So tackling between two relationships I found myself in a consistent tug of war, having Malik wanting family and Rico wanting to start a family with me. I couldn't juggle another relationship and because of it Lil Mexico was feeling some type of way.

"Damn boo, you're leaving again, to go hang with which one, Rico or Malik?" Lil Mexico sarcastically asked as she rolled her eyes.

Feeling the negative vibe early Friday morning as I finished payroll for the week, I grinned and responded, "Huh? Girl don't ask me no dumb shit, when you already know Malik is taking me and the kids shopping."

Frustrated, Lil Mexico snapped back, "You never want to hang out anymore, it's like you too busy for me, like I'm just here and you're always off doing your own thing." Feeling bad, I assured Lil Mexico that these weekend trips wouldn't be as often, but because I appreciate her loyalty to me and my business, that I would send her to bail bond school and pay to get her license. That was all she needed to hear. Satisfied at the arrangement she hugged me and giggled, "Don't get pregnant this weekend bitch! Don't worry you know I got your back, you're like a sister to me."

"You know you're the sister I never had, we're like Peanut Butter and Jelly." And just like that the office was back to its normal crazy routine. But later down the road I would find out the true meaning of royalty over loyalty when it came to friendships.

For almost a whole year I partied, shopped and took random trips out of the country with Rico and went to sporting events, family dinners and family trips out of town with Malik, not to mention keeping Lil Mexico happy. It was a constant job. I mean having to make up stories to the two niggas in my life when I couldn't be accounted for with one nigga because I was with the other, trying not to hurt anyone's feelings and wanting everyone to be happy. It was tiresome and when it finally came crashing down, I became public enemy number one to everyone in the circle, especially when Rico's charming ways turned into playing ways instead.

CHAPTER 5

Playing wifey to Malik and party chick to Rico had finally caught up with my ass when baby daddy played inspector gadget, pulling up while Rico was at my house. "Asia get your fucking ass to this door." Malik screamed at the top of his lungs, waking Rico and I up from our afternoon nap. *The fuck*, I thought, as my eyes got big and my heart began racing. I quickly pulled my pants over my fat ass and found one of Rico's tank tops on the floor, throwing it over my head.
"I know that nigga ain't down there banging on the fucking door like he the damn police!" Rico angrily yelled, trying to beat me to the front door.
"Baby, chill." I pleaded, "He'll go away in a minute," I tried to grab Rico's arm, pulling his hand back as he reached for the door handle.
"Let me fucking go Asia!" Rico snatched his hand back and within the blink of an eye, the door was opened. Within seconds, without the exchange of words, fists were being thrown. All I could do was stand in the doorway, not knowing what to do, tears streaming down my cheeks, unsure of who's side to take, I froze. *If I take Malik's side, I hurt Rico and I lose him, but taking Rico's side I go against my kids father and I can't do that.* Suddenly Malik's homeboy raced into my driveway and grabbed Malik with one hand and blind-sided Rico with a left hook.
"Nigga get the fuck back," Slim warned Rico, as he grabbed Malik now with both hands, "My nigga, chill, let's go you got fire in the car and we don't need the crackers coming."
Malik let go of Rico's throat, with fire in his eyes, stood up from on top of Rico and looked at me. Fury in his voice, "Bitch your dead to me and so are the kids, I hate you! Fuck you and that nigga!" As he stormed off into his car, I embraced Rico as I kneeled onto the ground, crying because Malik hated me and Rico had got beat up because of me. "Baby I'm so sorry," looking Rico in his eyes.

"Man that nigga dead, I swear, what the fuck Asia!" Rico pushed off me, his eye swollen and busted lip. With bloody spit coming from his mouth, Rico looked like a swollen raisin. That day I spent kissing Rico's ass, playing nurse to his battle wounds, while dealing with thoughts of Malik and how he felt about me. Feeling torn, I was hurt knowing that the man I laid down and had two kids with hated me and that my kids were going to suffer because of the choice I made, playing both sides of the field. For the next few days Rico and I stayed by each other's side, comforting each other, while Malik refused to call or reach out to his kids or even me, not even to cuss me out. Days passed and Rico had to get back on the road to handle things, leaving me and the kids alone. Trying to get through each day without thinking about only Malik only got worse. Then the nigga popped up at my office while I was out for lunch. Ripping files, smashing the flat screen TVs on the wall, throwing computers off the desks and pouring bleach into the security system. Lil Mexico tried pleading with him not to destroy the office, but Malik wasn't trying to hear any of that.
"Tell that bitch she's the enemy," Malik said as he walked out the door.
"Asia hurry up and get here, Malik went ape shit in the office." Lil Mexico franticly said into the phone, rushing over I walked in to what looked to be the aftermath of Hurricane Katrina, stepping on broken glass from the smashed TVs and dismantled computers. I felt so broken that Malik had struck yet again, first the shooting up of my car, now this.
"I can't believe this." I sobbed as I shook my head and scanned the entire office, trying to figure out where to start.
"Asia, mama, I am so sorry, like I couldn't stop Lik he was on a rampage." Lil Mexico said as she started to pick up ripped files from the floor. Then we started to smell a burning scent and a mixture of bleach. We turned our attention to the security system, and noticed it began to smoke from the security box.
"Hurry Mexi, go grab the fire extinguisher!" I shouted. Seconds later the smoke had smoldered and the white

chemical from the extinguisher now covered the floor in addition to everything else. A pit in my stomach began to form; I was devastated by the damage and even more devastated knowing Malik had done this. My mouth began to water; I knew I had to throw up. Running across files and bleach, I made it to the toilet and everything I had consumed in the past three days all came up. "Asia you good mama? Don't worry about the office, we'll just close it for a day or two," Lil Mexico added sarcastically. "We'll put a sign up that we're doing renovations to the office." Trying not to laugh, I splashed water onto my face and rinsed my mouth out with Listerine.

"Bitch you stupid." I joked walking out of the bathroom. "Well at least the nigga ain't go in the safe and shit he left the bathroom alone too." Deciding not to give any credit to my baby daddy for his latest attack, I didn't tell anyone what happened, not even Rico. *I mean the nigga already got beat up once, what the hell was he gonna do? Get beat up again. Fuck that! It's WAR.*

Knowing all his "business spots" which were really dope houses, I decided to drop a line to one of the city's biggest snakes, Kolya, a well-known jack boy. He made a living scheming and robbin' niggas. Seeing how there are no rules in street war and how this nigga Malik keep fucking up my stuff, I decided he would get a taste of his own medicine, so I sent Kolya to a major spot of his in Harlem. They say two wrongs don't make a right, but I believed in an eye for an eye and Malik got away with fucking with me for the last time. I mean this shit was deeper than just Rico, going back to this nigga having a baby on me, all the lies and cheating he did, why the fuck was he big mad about a nigga I started talking to after we broke up? So fucking what if I fucked Malik and spent time with him, shit I was just doing the same shit he did to me, but the only difference was Malik knew about Rico, so it wasn't top secret information.

Three weeks after I gave Kolya Malik's spot, I received a phone call at 7:16 in the morning. Malik's spot had been robbed and that two of his workers had got shot and one was

in critical condition. Malik was on a rampage once again, placing a $250,000 price on Kolya's head because the worker who got shot in the stomach, grabbed Kolya's mask off and recognized his face before he passed out. Six hours later that fat nigga woke up and told Malik everything and that Kolya came in shot the one nigga in the face, not knowing that there was another nigga in the house. Kolya had grabbed all the work and $327,000.00 outta the safe, by taking the nigga he shot over to the safe and used his thumb print to unlock it. The fat nigga then continued telling Malik that when Kolya walked passed the bathroom, that's when the fat nigga grabbed him from behind, trying to grab the .45 glock from Kolya which he was unsuccessful in doing. Kolya elbowed him in the face and turned around, but not before the fat nigga was able to grab his ski mask off his head. That's when Kolya shot the nigga three times in the stomach before running off. Sweat started to make its way down my forehead, knowing that if Malik got to Kolya before I did, he'd make the nigga tell him how he knew about that spot and if anyone was involved before he would kill him. Hanging up the phone, the feeling of panic started to set in, jumping outta my bed, I dialed Kolya's private number to see where he was at. "Hello, hello?" I said in the phone, trying to remain calm, "Where you at, you straight?"
There was a brief pause and finally Kolya responded, "Yeah a nigga straight. I just fucked up, letting that fat fuck get my mask." sounding defeated he went on to say, "Man I heard your people put a price on my head. I'm already out the way shorty, see ya when I see ya." The phone hung up, unsure of why this nigga was terrified at the thought of Malik catching up with him, I tried calling back, it went straight to voicemail. After calling the number back twenty-three times, I gave up. Thirty minutes later the nanny arrived to get the children ready and off to school, I hauled ass in my baby beamer, not even knowing where I was going. I just drove, riding down Martin Luther King Blvd, the hood seemed cold, nothing but dark tinted cars roamed the neighborhood and that usually meant jack boys and killers were on the scene. When I pulled into my office building parking lot I was shook. The uncertainly of

what the future held for me and not knowing where the fuck Kolya was set, I felt sick to the stomach I grabbed the steering wheel with both hands and my head down I heard a *Tap! Tap!* on my driver window, I jumped, letting out some pee, looked at my window, it was just Lil Mexico. "Bitch OMG! You scared the shit outta me, the fuck." I cried, holding my heart with my right hand as I opened the driver door with my left. "My bad hoe," she giggled, "Man you heard bout Malik's spot and the nigga they said who did it, bitch talk about karma," Lil Mexico exclaimed.
"Yeah, I can't even believe it." I said rolling my eyes.

Days passed and still no sign of Kolya or his whereabouts and everyday I double checked my surroundings, not knowing if Malik would be lurking in the brushes somewhere waiting for me. Then finally my questions were answered. Watching the 5 o'clock news sitting on my sofa in the living room, Kolya's name appeared on the on the TV screen and the news anchor stated, "Keenan Thomas, a three-time convicted felon is leading police in a high-speed chase, after police attempted to pull him over for a traffic stop because the tag on the vehicle does not match what the DMV had. Thomas shot at the police and took off." *Oh my freakin God,* I said to myself, *This dumb ass nigga been here in town the whole fucking time, stupid dumb fuck, the police just need to kill his stupid ass or else I will.* I was glued to the television screen. Forty-five minutes later, the police shot out his back tires to the 2016 Dodge Magnum he was driving and the chase had ended, surrounded by SWAT and the local police department on I-75, Kolya was done and so was I, I thought, until Kolya opened the front door and shot at the police again, this time he was out numbered and was shot and killed instantly. The news anchor quickly got back on the screen, "We here at NBC-2 apologize to viewers for the graphic image and we also like to apologize to the family members of the assailant." Powering the television off, I was shocked. *Damn that's crazy but shit a closed mouth can't tell shit.* A feeling of relief came across me, standing up from the sofa, it felt like a weight was lifted

from my shoulders, granted I felt bad about the situation, but one dead person is better than two.
Kolya was gone but Malik was still pissed with me. My children started to ask where their daddy was and why hadn't he come to see them. Unsure of what to tell them, I just told them that their daddy had to go outta town to handle business and that I wasn't sure when he'd be back. Feeling guilty that I was the reason why their daddy wasn't coming to see them, I reached out to Malik's mom, trying to reconcile any piece of Lik's heart to see his kids, his mom just told me, "You know how Malik is Asia and although I don't get involved in ya'll bullshit, you hurt my son and I don't know when his hard-headed ass will come around. Just give him some more time." We hung up our phones, and at that point I couldn't do anything but accept that answer and stop trying to reach out to him. A week later I received a notice by a process server at my office to appear in court. The nigga put himself on child support.

CHAPTER 6

Brand new furnishings, Apple computers, and a few new Sony flat screen televisions back on the wall, not to mention a fresh coat of cherry wood and eastern grey paint and the installation of a high-end security system, along with an electric lock and buzzer on the entrance door, my bail bond office doors opened back up, with a brand-new attitude. Now that the drama with Malik and Kolya was over, things around town were back to being peaceful and I was able to focus on my business, especially since Rico found himself more and more on the road, lessening our time together. I was ok with that since I sent Lil Mexico to bail school to get her license. Being in the office more I found time to hustle inmates to get them out of jail, once again pissing off other bail bond companies. *Fuck it,* I thought, *I've been outta the office long enough, it's time to stir shit up and get back on my grind game.* Pretty face, slim waist and fat ass, I made my way back and forth to the jail for two straight weeks, in my waist high jeans and bodysuit, with my Giuseppe Zanotti Coline Wings. My presence was felt, as other bail agents frowned when I entered the jail.

"*There that bitch goes. How is she still in business when her baby daddy is a criminal? I can't stand her fake bougie ass!*" Hilarious! I knew that ran through their mind and I loved it. Seeing them hating on me didn't offend me and that's what these companies failed to understand. Matter of fact it just drove me that much harder. Whether you loved me or hated me, respect was ALWAYS given. "Hey hun, see business is going good for you." a bail agent coldly said as if she was forced.

"Hey boo, you know I'm trying, one bond at a time." I smiled proudly and strutted right beside her. The agent rolled her eyes, as she walked out the jail lounge, but not before I stopped her by saying, "I'm sure I'll see you back down here sweetie, have a blessed day." One thing about me, I knew how to play both sides of the field, I can be 'nice nasty' in a

professional setting or I can just be like 'fuck you' in the streets.
Meanwhile Rico was starting to act a little suspicious by his dismissive demeanor. I mean don't get me wrong the little break we had from each other was necessary given the previous drama, but shit it was the third week and the nigga was still giving me the cold shoulder. I decided when Lil Mexico came back from bail school I was gonna take a short leave of absence to sneak up on Rico in his South Beach condo. The nigga acted like he was busy and couldn't come see me.

It was late night on a Friday, I had packed a weekend bag and was speeding down I-75 towards Miami, jamming to YFN Lucci 'Wish Me Well.' An hour and a half later I was pulling into Rico's driveway and behind a parked car I had never seen before. Sitting in the car, ignition pushed off, it seemed like a thousand possibilities ran through my head and before I knew it, I had popped open my trunk and had my steel metal baseball bat in my hand. I took a deep breath and prepared myself for what I imagined I'd be walking into. Pushing the elevator button several times, I felt like my heart was going to burst. When the elevator doors finally opened one of Rico's neighbors walked out, it was a female, she shook her head as she looked down at the baseball bat and softly said, "Girl I don't blame you." Before I could ask what she meant, her boyfriend grabbed her arm firmly and whispered what seemed like, "That shit ain't our business." I watched as the couple walked off as the elevator doors closed. My hands were shaking; I could feel my ears get hot from the pure anticipation of seeing a dusty ass hoe in his house.
The elevator doors opened and I walked to the door which held the destiny for Rico and whatever bum ass bitch he had in there. Walking up the door, I stood there for a moment and put my left ear to the door to see if I could hear anyone talking. *No, nothing... dammit. Fuck it Asia, get the key from under the plant and just go in!* I retrieved the key and quietly unlocked the door and flung open the door. My eyes were bugged out in

anticipation for what I might see. I busted through the door and there was Rico standing there in the open kitchen with his hands in the sink and nothing but boxers on. I took no time to start in with the questions. "Where the fuck she at bitch?" Without letting Rico get a word in, I continue the interrogation, "Oh what nigga you can't hear now? Nigga I'm speaking a different language?" Scanning the room, I didn't find a purse, a pair of heels; shit not even a hair tie. "Fuck you bitch, don't you even wanna speak? You so fucking busy in the kitchen in your fucking boxers!"

Rico stood there with a dazed and confused look on his face, then a figure appeared in the laundry room doorway behind Rico. I instinctively raised my bat high, ready to smash this nigga and that hoe's face in, but then the figure came in full view. It was another nigga! "Huh? The fuck…" I choked on my words.

"Asia it's not what it looks like!" Rico pleaded, as he slowly walked toward me.

"The fuck it ain't. Why the fuck this nigga in his fucking boxers, with a fucking wig on!?" I screamed in horror. Tears beginning to run down my face in anger, then the nigga spoke with a big ass Kool-Aid smile on his face.

"Well Rico you gonna tell her why I'm in my boxers?" smirking as he crossed his arms.

"Shut up Darius!" Rico demanded taking his eyes away from me, then quickly diverting his attention back to my bat and me.

"You're fucking gay Rico? No fucking wonder you knew how to treat a female, you're a damn punk!" Tears flowing from eyes, it took every fucking thing for me not to split this flaw, punk ass bitch face, "Punk bitch! I should've let Malik stomp your shit in!" Disgusted, I walked backwards to the front door, my heart trying to jump outta my chest, down Rico's throat to suffocate his ass. I made my way out of the front door to the elevator and as the doors closed I could hear Rico yelling, "Asia I'm sorry, don't," and before he could finish his words the elevator doors closed. I slumped against the rail of the elevator, dropped the bat and sobbed hysterically, not because

I was sad, but rather sick and humiliated by Rico's gay truth. *Asia, how could be you a fucking a ...?! If anyone finds out, I'll be the fucking laughing stock of the community!* I shook my head while I scolded myself walking past Rico's car, devastated and pissed the hell off. Without even thinking I busted out the driver side window to Rico's Bentley, then the back window, along with his tail lights. I felt better in that moment as I looked back at the havoc I'd caused to this nigga's car. I couldn't help get his bitch's car too. *Fuck it, I hope this nigga finds his car fucked up funny too*, I said to myself throwing the bat in my back seat. I fixed my hair and backed out of Rico's parking garage and that was the last I seen of Rico.

My personal life was fucked up, finding out my boyfriend was actually gay and Malik beyond pissed off and angry, I found myself alone. Although we shared 50/50 custody, Malik kept the kids the majority of the time and hell I couldn't blame him, especially with the information I knew about Rico. It was best to agree to whatever Malik wanted. Meanwhile, as if shit couldn't get worse, Lil Mexico took it upon herself to manage the office while I was busy dealing with all my bullshit, work was the last thing on my mind. She claimed she needed help, so she hired some bum ass street hoe, whom supposedly was her cousin, into the office. Although I was irritated at the thought of some random in my office, I couldn't really say much, shit I was barely there and Lil Mexico was busy posting bonds and handling business since she'd received her license, hell she was doing my job.

Six months after Lil Mexico hired her 'cousin' the Department of Financial Services made an unexpected visit into my office. I was sitting at my desk, going over bonds and payments when in walked Ms. Beth Ann Saucey, the biggest bitch in the department and someone you didn't want to piss off either. I'm talking about this old lady gets a damn hard on every time she sees me. Ever since I opened up my office, a young, beautiful, talented, popular boss bitch like myself, she's been out to get me. Although all the other times were bogus, this time was a little bit more serious, the bitch had me. While dealing with gay ass Rico, I was allowing Lil Mexico complete full access of my entire office and little did I know the sneaky bitch had her cousin writing fake receipts and stealing money from clients and Ms. Saucey with her saggy titties and chipped front tooth, had all the receipts to prove it. "Damn Lil Mexico, what the fuck were you thinking?" I screamed hysterically. I could feel the fury from within building with full force. I could have jumped across my desk and choked this bitch out. All she did was sit in the chair across from me with a dumb look on her face. "Stupid bitch you knew that this would come back on me! After everything I've done for you, selfish ass Mexican."

Barely able to get a word in Lil Mexico pleaded, "Asia, I'm so sorry, I swear I didn't know!"

I knew that bitch was lying, "Get the fuck out of my office you and your bitch-ass, thief-ass, fake-ass cousin!" I demanded. As the front door closed, I fell to my knees in disbelief that a friend of mine would steal from me. This pocket watching ass hoe really played me, after everything we had been through, she crossed me. The hurt I endured that day was worse than catching Rico gay ass or when Malik's side bitch came to my daughter's birthday party. Lil Mexico was like a sister, someone who knew everything about me. I shared my entire world with her, but even the massive hurt I felt would not prepare me for what Ms. Saucey had up her sleeve. Two weeks after she brought her arrogant ass into my office, she came back, but not by herself this time with two uniformed officers. She charged me with larceny and extortion of services because many clients were paying double for their bonds. On May 9th, I was arrested and made every fucking television news program. The media ate it up, making it seem like I was stealing thousands of dollars from my clients like I was some bum ass hoe pressed for money. I was totally embarrassed. I was released on a $500,000 bond. Malik came to my rescue, posted bail and even picked me up from the jail house. Smiling as I walked out the double doors of the jailhouse, I ran to him, like a kid running to the ice cream truck, and hugged him tightly, grateful and happy to see him,

Malik, hugged me back and gently gave a kiss on my forehead and slowly said, "Bitch I'm still mad at you, but I still love you and our kids need you." The tears continued rolling down my face. I looked up at Malik, wiping the snot from my nose with my sleeve, I responded, "I love you too."

Following my arrest, rumors started to circulate that Lil Mexico had set the whole thing up. This raggedy ass hoe was bragging around town that she was sick of my shit and she could take over the bail game, by getting me out. *What a scum bitch, play back is a bitch,* I thought to myself. My license was temporary suspended, and I waited, praying the charges would be dropped. I was stressed the fuck out, I was like a ticking time bomb and little did I know, that bomb was about to go off.

CHAPTER 7

365 Bail Bonds was the name of Lil Mexico's bail agency that she opened one month after she attempted to sabotage my business. I was fucking livid and as crazy as it seemed, Malik was there for me, forewarning me that I would get into bigger trouble than I already was and it wasn't worth it. Not to mention he warned me that he wasn't dropping anymore money on my attorney's fees if I did some dumb shit. So fuck it, I let her go for the time being and found another agent to use their license to keep my business open, since my shit was screwed up. Jalissa, a Latin American came through and posted bonds for me and assisted with office work. I was extremely grateful, although I heard that she and Malik had a past, I didn't give a damn, hell I was already in a jam and I was in no position to be picky or petty. Little did I know, shit was ugly and was about to get uglier.

Feeling defeated at my own game with the slick move Lil Mexico pulled, I was vulnerable but pressed to prove a point to anyone who thought I was off my shit. Two weeks after my license was officially suspended, my homeboy who I bonded out awhile back hit my line about a paid hosting job for his upcoming concert. *Shit why not,* I thought, *the perfect reason to get cute for these hating ass hoes and no good niggas and get cut a check for it.* My BeBe dress looked like it was painted on. Louis Vuitton on my feet, and my Chanel lip gloss had my lips looking like Kylie Jenner, I was ready. But don't get my swag confused, I was on my rich girl shit, but kept a bottle of mace in my clutch. Cardi B was blasting in the house. Anika, my homegirl of ten years and my hairdresser poured shots of Patron, as Mimi my gangsta bitch from elementary snap chatted her ass off. "Asia your security and limo driver have arrived," Ms. Mary, the nanny yelled. She was excited because she hated Cardi B music and she was ready for some peace and quiet, she hated when I turnt up.

Escorted from the entry way of my home to the limo, our security guard was fine as shit, looking like Idris Elba, tall dark and handsome with grown man confidence. He wore a loud layer of cologne. I loved the smell of Creed. I could've melted in his hands; that fragrance was my biggest weakness. Loud music and alcohol, we were lit and forty-five minutes later we arrived, pulling up like some damn celebrities. Security opened the door to our limo and we gracefully stepped out, all eyes on us as if we were the performers. Bitches staring us down from head to toe, as they waited in line, looking annoyed. Niggas standin' in line lickin' their lips, trying to catch eye contact. I swear I lived for that moment. We entered the club, with security pushing on lookers aside, we had our stank walk on, ass wobbling from side to side, our hair swinging, left to right as it brushed the top of our asses, we really were a sight to see. Making our way to the reserved VIP section, the club was so swole and the section we were in allowed us to overlook the entire club from upstairs. Soon the bottle girls made their way to our section, holding up the Ace of Spades signs and sparklers. I looked into the crowd and locked eyes with a familiar face. Mother fucking Rico was in the club, looking like a million dollars with his Balencia shoes and Balmain jeans and shirt. That nigga looked good and gay to me all at the same time. I rolled my eyes and he smiled, I turned my back and snap chatted the bottle girls as they made their way to the table. Booty bumping to the music, we were jamming. I was feeling myself and tipsy as hell. I was in my zone, until I was tapped on my shoulder and turned around to stand face to face to Rico. Unbothered, I started to grind my fat ass all over his dick, laughing to myself knowing that this nigga was pie. Not to mention no one knew what I did and watching the thirsty hoes study Rico's every move, I decided to give them a show. *Fuck it,* I said to myself. Towards the end of the night, with two bottles of Patron empty and a half of bottle of Hennessy left, our security signaled to us, that it was time to depart.

"I miss you," whispered Rico in my ear, "I fucked up and that wasn't me, I miss us." looking like a sad puppy dog.

I smiled "I just gave the audience what they wanted to see, but nothing changes between us, boo kitty." *The hell this nigga*

thought, he was acting like I caught him cheating on me with a bitch. Amused at the fact, I knew this nigga's dirty little secret while these bitches were so quick to want to jump in the bed with him. As we got ready to exit the back way out the club, I caught Mane Mane, Malik's homeboy peeping at me, smiling and shaking his head. I awkwardly looked at him, unsure of what the fuck he was shaking his head at. My thought process was at an all-time slow, I ignored it and walked off with my girls and security, leaving Rico bitch ass in the section.
"Girl tonight don't owe me shit Asia! I'm talking about niggas were begging for our attention!" Anika was drunk laughing as she flopped her fat ass in the back of the limo.
"I swear, I had so much fun, it was all eyes on us," Meme yelled in my face as I sat in the limo smirking. I sipped on my champagne flute, tipsy as hell. By this time all our phones were blowing up with niggas trying to shoot their shot in our DM and some through texts, the shit was hilarious. *So predictable,* I thought. Feeling confident and sexy, flattered by all the attention, I wasn't ready for what came next.
So you still fucking that fuck boy huh? Why you needed my help for fucking attorneys? I let you fuck me and you back in public with this lame ass bitch! I could hear Malik's voice; I felt his anger through the text message. It sent chills down my arms and back.
I quickly responded, *what are you talking about? I didn't know he was going to show up! I love you, I want to be with you, can I come over?* I pleaded in my text. I felt a tingling feeling; it was hot. Now I was completely numb, I instructed the limo driver to take me home first.
Anika started to trip, "Girl what the hell, I know you ain't get me drunk only to go home bitch."
"Listen boo kitty something came up with Lik, I gotta go. I'll make it up, promise" I stepped out of the open limo door. The driver gently grabbed my hand and escorted me to my front door. I took a soothing bath and rubbed my body down with Versace body cream. I laid in my bed just staring at the ceiling, wondering what Malik was going to do. I knew he was mad. *I can't believe bitch ass Mane Mane went back and told*

Lik that bullshit. Damn that's a fuck nigga. Unable to fall asleep, I rolled over and the clock read 4:02 a.m. I got out of bed and made my way to my bathroom and into the medicine cabinet, where I found a 10mg of Percocet. I popped a whole one and looked up at the mirror, *Damn girl get yourself together, man fuck Malik. You got more important shit to be stressing about, girl you could lose your bail license. What then?* Feeling broken and sad, but not wanting to call anyone, especially at that time of morning, I cried myself to sleep. Sunday afternoon I finally opened my eyes to seventeen text messages and fifty-two missed phone calls. All of them were nothing but niggas trying to holler and jailhouse calls of people wanting a three-way. Later that evening I finally got a response from Malik, "Meet me at the spot so you can get the kids."
"Okay," I thought, *well at least he said something.* I threw on a fitted Pink outfit, slid my Givenchy slides on and jumped into my Benz. Feeling anxious, I sped down the highway. When I arrived at the spot, Malik's Audi was already parked, so I pulled up. He immediately opened his front door and hopped out. He walked calmly to my driver side window and said, "Aye I need to holler at cha about my kids." I watched Malik walk over to my passenger side door, I was confused. His passenger door opened and my son and daughter got out walking towards my car. I wasn't paying attention to Malik, I didn't see his face as he opened the passenger door and before I knew it, he grabbed my hair and had pulled me into the passenger chair, "Bitch you think it's sweet, pussy ass hoe to keep embarrassing me with that fuck boy!" Malik's voice was full of rage.
I begged him to stop, "Please! Please! I'm sorry, I didn't know he was going to be..." Malik punched me in my mouth. I began to taste my blood. I fell apart when I heard my son scream in horror, "Daddy, daddy stop!"
I glimpsed over at my kids to see my son holding onto his sister, shielding her. "Malik let me go," screaming at the top of my lungs. I used my left foot to push on the horn, trying to get a nearby driver's attention.

"Hoe you did this bitch!" Malik hit me once more, this time in the eye, then he let go of my weave, which thankfully was sewn into my scalp. Malik jumped into his car, wheels screeching, and just like that he was gone. Now don't get me wrong, Malik and I have had our boxing moments, but never in front of our children and that's because he never wanted the children to see him disrespect their mother, *crazy I know but I always respected that about him*. Devastated and upset, trying to pull myself together as my children got into the car, blood dripping from my top lip. My son sobbed, "Mommy I'm sorry."

I felt even more upset, I turned to my son, rubbing the back of his head gently, "Baby it's nothing you could've done, daddy is just upset with mommy right now," I kissed his forehead and grabbed my daughter's hand as she cried in the backseat and softly said, "It's going to be ok mommy's princess." I readjusted the rear-view mirror and put the car in drive. During that ride home I turned on the radio for a much needed distraction. 105.5 slow jams was playing, R. Kelly's *When a woman's fed up* and that shit did something to me. I was emotionally drained from the baby daddy drama, to catching Rico's punk ass, to getting played by Lil Mexico. I was pissed and tired of people thinking they could just get over on me, especially people who I considered family, or the ones I was intimate with whether it was sexually or whom I shared my deepest, darkest secrets with. I pulled up in the driveway and sat there, feeling uneasy and anxious all at the same time. I sent the children inside to get fed and bathed, since the nanny was already waiting on their arrival. "Now mommy's lil babies, please don't tell anyone that daddy hurt mommy, ok? We don't want daddy to get in trouble."

"Ok," both children responded, as they shut the car doors and walked towards the house. I dialed 9-1-1. I was nervous as hell, I had to talk myself into pressing the green button on my iPhone. *Asia, this nigga just put his hands on you in front of the kids, he don't give a damn about you or the kids! Spare his ass for what? Yeah you ain't no cop calling, police ass bitch, but fuck that, you gotta show him. Bitch ya'll ain't even together, bet he don't try that other bitch of a baby mama he got!* Next thing I knew the 9-1-1 dispatcher was on the line and I was giving Malik's full name, "Malik Micah Mitchell." For some reason I still felt a sense of protection for this nigga, I refused to give his address I pretended like I didn't know, although I knew they didn't believe me.

A few weeks later I was still battling the whole bail license situation. Eventually the attorneys came to a resolution, a resolution I wasn't in complete agreement to. They ordered my license to be in suspension for 180 days, along with mandating a moral ethics bail bond course and 300 community service hours. I was so annoyed. "Asia it's either this or go to trial and the possibly of winning is 50/50," Attorney Shultz advised me.

"Fine." I rolled my eyes and signed on the dotted line, I felt defeated, but in a sense relieved because at least there was light at the end of the tunnel and I would regain my license. *One fight down, a few more to go, baby daddy and Lil Mexico,* well at least that's what I told myself. November 25th at 4:43 a.m. a text message came thru and at 8:15 that morning I rolled over and opened my notifications. Nothing would have prepared me for this one. An unknown number had texted me, I opened it and read *Please do not respond, I just thought you should know this.* I scrolled further a saw an attachment that needed to be downloaded, unsure if it was some bullshit ass spam or virus, I hesitated for a moment, then said *fuck it.* I clicked on download and waited for what seemed like forever for it to finally load, it was a video and I pressed play. Mortified and feeling sick to my stomach, I dropped my phone onto the bedroom rug. Now remember when I told you, that the agent who I had working in my office was rumored to have had a past with Malik. Well, let me just say it was no longer considered a past. The video contained Malik and Jalissa fucking in my office three nights ago. He was filming her sucking his dick and then him fucking her from the back on my fucking desk! I could not fucking believe the audacity of this nigga. My chest was caving in, I felt like I was having a panic attack. I started to pace back and forth in my bedroom, tears of anger flooded down my cheeks. I tried to calm myself down, but I couldn't. I was enraged. All I could see was red and I wanted blood. I picked up my phone from the floor and called Anika. "Bitch, I need you to ride with me, this pussy ass hoe is gonna get taught a lesson," I yelled angrily in the phone.

"Damn bitch calm down, come through and scoop me, I got cha," Anika replied.

Honk! Honk! I layed on the horn until Anika brought her ass outside and into my car. "Bitch I see great minds think alike, who is that in all that black?" Anika laughed. I hauled ass down the street. Mace in my hand and a baseball bat in Anika's, we pulled up to my office. As expected Jalissa's car was parked in front of the building with no other cars in sight. "You ready?" I asked Anika.

"Bitch you know I was born ready," Anika said firmly, no longer on joke time we were on straight business. We walked quickly up to the front door, I flung it open with one hand, mace in the other behind my back. Jalissa was sitting at her desk, surprised, with a dumb look on her face. She was trying to figure out why Anika had a baseball bat in her hand.

"Hey girl, damn do we have a pick up to do," she nervously asked.

"Naw boo kitty, but you thought a bitch was sweet, like I wasn't gonna find out about you sucking on Malik's dick bitch!" I swung at the bitch and missed! She tried to run, but the hoe wasn't fast enough, I grabbed her by her Brazilian nappy ass weave and maced the hoe in the face, "Hoe you tried me!" I screamed as I threw the mace on the ground and then punched her several times in the face. Jalissa tried to cover the blows, she fell and next thing I knew I was on top of her. Anika watched the front door to make sure no one was coming up. I slammed her head on the floor, until I saw blood. "Bitch chill boo, don't kill the bitch!" Anika yelled as she started to pull me off of her. I snapped out of it, and this hoe was laid out on the ground, crying and pleading for forgiveness. I turned to hold onto the desk to catch my breath and Anika walked backed to the front door to scout the parking lot. All of a sudden, I felt a sharp pain in my back. I turned around and was greeted with a pair of scissors, inches away from my face. I blocked the shiny blade with my arm, and before I knew it blood was everywhere. I saw Anika swing the bat at the back of Jalissa's head and then I blacked out.

I woke up in a hospital bed with police officers in my face. Dazed and confused I looked around for a familiar face. *Where the fuck is Anika?* I looked down and saw my arm wrapped up. "Ma'am, my name is nurse Kay, how are you feeling?" The young African American Megan Good looking ass nurse said softly.
"I'm ok, what's going on?" I asked.
"Well Asia, you were in a physical altercation and you were attacked with scissors to your back and arm, as a matter of fact, the doctor is going to come in to assess the damage in both your back and arm." Suddenly I heard a familiar voice, my mother.
"Asia Asia?" She kept asking, until she was directly into my room, eyes full of tears, my mother was shocked to see all the blood on my clothes and confused by the situation. "Baby are you ok? Oh my God Asia, what the hell happened? I could kill this bitch who did this," unconcerned by the police officers standing by the doorway, my mother was livid.
"Mom I'm ok, my fucking arm is killing me. I can't even unbandage my arm it hurts so much," tears started to stream down my face. I started to feel the pain because my body wasn't pumping adrenaline anymore. Now all I felt was pain and regret. "Mom where's Anika?"
"Anika went to jail for some battery charge, that bitch is trying to press charges on both you and her!" My mother responded angrily, "But don't worry Asia, Lil Mexico is going to take care of it." *The fuck!* I thought, giving my mom a dumbass look. She further explained, "Asia listen Lil Mexico came out here earlier but they wouldn't allow her back here. She's the one who told me that Anika had got locked up. Baby I know you hurt by the shit Lil Mexico did, but she told me that she

was sorry. She texted me and told me that she'd be back out here shortly after she posts Anika's bond and she's not gonna have Anika pay the bond either." my mother explained. I felt uneasy about the situation, but I was thankful that Anika was gonna be taken care of. I damn sure didn't want my girl in jail. The doctors finally arrived with a team of nurses. They requested my mother leave the room as the doctor would be taking a look at my arm. I was feeling nervous as the doctor removed the bandage on my back and requested to have the stab wound numbed. Peeping the room and all the nurses circled around my bed, I started to question the doctor. "What's going on doctor, matter of fact can I get a picture of my back to see what the hell it looks like?" The doctor smiled and without hesitation asked for my phone I quickly handed it over. *Click! Click!* She handed it back to me, I was instructed to hold still, then I felt a needle in my back and I yelled in pain. It made my wound burn. "What the HELL?" I was pissed. Each of the nine nurses began to lean in grabbing my arms, even the one that was fucked up. Next thing I knew I heard, *Bang! Bang! Bang!*

They were stapling the wound! I sat there numb, but my heart was racing because the sound of staples, it felt weird as shit and I couldn't move my arms to move away from the stapler. It felt like I was being detained. The doctor shot me another smile showcasing her shiny Veneers, and quietly asked me, "That didn't hurt, did it?" Feeling like I was being set up, I shook my head no. "Now I'm just going to take a look at your arm." I began to cry and pleaded with the doctor not to hurt me, "Please. Please be careful!" I cried out. I could feel the pressure of each nurse's grip getting tighter. The doctor unraveled the bandage and calmly ordered the nurses, "Hold her down." Before I could get a word in edge wise, the sound of the staples echoed through the emergency room. I cried, screamed and hollered in pain; everyone on the emergency floor could hear my cries. Feeling faint & light headed from the adrenaline and immense pain, I passed out. I woke up shortly after still in the hospital bed. At first, I thought I had awakened from a horrible nightmare until I seen my mother's

face. She had tears streaming down her rosy cheeks and pain written all over her face. I knew this wasn't a dream. No longer feeling pain from my arm, I quickly glanced, it looked like something from a horror film. Disgusted, I put the hospital blanket over it. I was drained and felt helpless. I laid in silence, counting the holes in the hospital ceiling, until another familiar voice filled the room. Meme walked in.
"Oh my God, bitch!" Meme gasped as she walked over, unaware of my mother's presence. "Girl the whole fucking city is talking about you and about that bum bitch Jalissa!" Meme shouted loudly, trying to peep my injuries.
"Yeah girl," I responded slowly, not really in the mood for the shits right now and what people were saying.
"Umm Asia really doesn't need to be bothered with that right now. Don't you think?" My mother chimed in.
"Oh snap! Yes ma'am, sorry didn't know you were sitting there." Meme said apologetically.
"Girl it's straight, the streets gonna talk," I said, winking at Meme, knowing that she didn't mean any harm by it.
"Girl this Anika," Meme responded as her text went off, "Her ass is on the way up here," Meme informed. "Dammit sorry for cursing," she said looking over at my mom. A little annoyed and exhausted, my mother excused herself from the room and left to grab some coffee down the hall. As soon as she stepped out the room, Meme had a whole damn ear full of shit to say. "Bitch the streets got you blowed up, liked you all handcuffed to the bed and shit and that hoe cut your arm off, bitch shit is crazy. And they say supposedly that bitch is up here at the hospital too with a broken nose, bruised ribs and that the hoe had a concussion from when Anika hit her with the baseball bat! Hoe ya'll some fucking savages! Why the fuck you ain't call me bitch, you know I would've rode with ya'll?" Meme continued on, "Look bitch Facebook is going in," she scrolled down her timeline all I could see was my name, Anika and that whore Jalissa's name in the comments. Unbothered at the moment, I told Meme to call Anika and see where she was at. But before the last number could be dialed, in walked Anika. Tears all down her face, she rushed in still

with the jailhouse bracelet on and hugged the hell outta my neck.
Filled with emotions, we both began to cry hysterically, "Bitch," Anika cried.
"Bitch!" I cried back, so relieved to see my bestie outta jail in the hospital room, all the shit Meme was telling me about was out the door. Both wiping each other's tears we just sat there, a smile even came across my face, which was quickly removed as my mom walked back into my room, pacing back and forth, as though she was about to fight one of us.
"What's going on ma?" I asked cautiously, unaware and confused from the change of attitude.
"You know that fuck nigga is here?!" She asked harshly as she eyeballed Meme and Anika.
"Who? Mom calm down." I said softly.
"Fucking Malik is in the room with that bitch Jalissa down the fucking hall. That's why there's so many police!" My mom exploded.
"What?" Anika said as she rose from her chair and gave a side eye to Meme to motion her to the door.
"What? Wait." I questioned as my eyes grew big and began to fill with tears. "He's here with her?" Feeling like a weak little girl, I didn't even stop Anika and Meme as they scurried down the hall, only to be forced out by the uniformed police officers. I could hear their shouts, "You fuck nigga!"
"Pussy ass hoe, I'll see you in the streets"
"Pussy ass hoe ass nigga, bitch made punk!" Then there was a faint yell to me "Asia we got you!" As I sat there feeling numb to this whole situation now, questioning myself in silence like, *why would he do this? Come to the hospital and not even check on the mother of his child? He hates me that much?* I asked the Lord to strengthen my heart and remove the pain I had. I grabbed hold of my mother's shirt and cried loudly, not wanting other patients or hospital personnel to hear me. My mother rubbed the back of my head and repeatedly assured me everything would be okay. Feeling pathetic and foolish, I felt like I could just die from the stress of it all, and over a man

who couldn't even come see about me. The hurt I felt at that moment was unbearable and sickened me to the core.
Feeling at my lowest point, I just closed my eyes and allowed the pain medicine to kick in through my IV. A few hours, still in the same bed, same room, I woke back up to a surgeon and his assistant in my room explaining to my mother the procedure I was about to undergo. I murmured, "Another surgery? No doctor, I can't go thru the pain!"
"No hun, you're going to be put to sleep. I have to go in your arm to repair the tendon damage you underwent. You'll wake back up in your bed." The doctor gently assured me. At this point I didn't care, I just wanted to be home and most importantly to see my babies. My heart had been ruptured and my physical injuries had the city running their lies, hell someone blogged that my arm was amputated, laid in the bed, waiting to be transferred to the surgery center of the hospital. Then, to add to my demise in walks Lil Mexico with a bouquet of yellow daisies, my favorite, with a 'Get Well' balloon attached to it. "Hey Asia, I know you probably don't wanna see me, but at the end of the day you were like a sister to me and I hate to see you like this," she said slowly. She even allowed a fake tear to surface.
Rolling my eyes, she was the last person I wanted to see, "Thank you hun, I know Asia appreciates them, it's just been a long day for her, I know you understand," my mother responded for me. Confused as to why the bitch was here and what the hell she wanted from me, I directed all my hurt and anger towards her now. I felt like I was only in this situation because she had crossed me. I stared at her with an ice glare. She felt my drift, because she started talking to my mom, "I swear, I never wanted this for Asia and although what's done is done, I want to be here for her and the kids. This situation has gotten completely out of hand and I can't believe what Malik is doing right now." She tried to sound remorseful, but my mother didn't bite, she just nodded her head in agreement. Eventually Lil Mexico picked up on our vibe and quietly left. Two days after my surgery and a shit load of pain meds I was feeling loopy as shit and alone. Although my girls were

around checking on me and that damn Anika was calling and coming through every hour on the hour, I was grateful, but shit that wasn't what I needed. I needed Malik. Feeling sorry for myself, I spent the majority of the next few days drowning in meds and sleeping. I'd wake up to hundreds of texts, from friends to strangers trying to be nosey and figure out what was going on. A week had passed and still, no communication with Malik. I was tired of hearing the bullshit the streets were saying so I decided to turn my cell phone off. Laying there I started to question myself and everything that had taken place, even thinking about Kolyon and the part I had played in that. I was trying to piece my life together, looking at the decisions I'd made. In that moment, I felt my life had spiraled out of control. Who the fuck was I becoming? From going back to Rico and the bullshit that happened with him, finding out he was fucking gay, to Lil Mexico playing me right under my nose, all the way to hiring Jalissa knowing my gut said her and Malik had something going on. I had no fucking control of myself. I didn't want to talk to anyone, because I didn't want to hear anyone's opinion.

CHAPTER 8

Eighteen hours later, I walked through the double doors with my attorney on my left, and my mom on my right. They tried their best to shield me, there was a ton of press awaiting an exclusive from the *Local Thug Bail Bondsman Facing Aggravated Battery*. "Is it that damn serious?" I asked fixing my hair in the back-seat mirror of my driver's suburban. "This is getting way out of hand," my mother responded. "Asia as your friend and attorney, I advise not to say anything to anyone regarding this case." Zac instructed, and I nodded in agreement. I closed my eyes as we headed to my house. *How the fuck did I get here? Where did I go wrong? Lord please place your hands on me and lead me out of this storm.* The truck stopped and when I opened eyes, my babies were running to the truck screaming, "Mommy!" Tears streamed down my eyes as I hugged them tightly, feeling overwhelmed I sobbed uncontrollably as I was led into the house. When inside I thanked Zac once again and he assured me things would get handled, then he saw himself out the front door. I turned to my mom, hugged and thanked her for her strength and for always being there.

As days turned to nights and nights to days, I sat in my home realizing I'd never taken the time to appreciate my life. I had such a beautiful home and all the hard work I put into it. It felt like I was walking through the house for the first time. "Damn I never appreciated this shit before," I said quietly as I shook my head. I always thought if I never bragged about certain things that would be considered being humble, but really I taught myself to never appreciate anything. Looking at pictures of me and my children, I felt like a failure. *How could I have let my children down, even my mom, the only person who genuinely cared for me and my well-being?* At that point I decided to hide myself to the world. I mean don't get shit twisted, my business was still being ran, my mother took over and handled all the business affairs, hiring new staff and making sure shit was ran properly. I was scrolling on my IG page, looking at pictures of me and Rico and all the parties and trips we had taken. I posted pictures almost every other day. I had over two thousand posts of outfits, clubs and designer shit; nothing about my kids and my business except some old shit from over a year ago. *Damn Asia, you really been on some shit.* I reminisced about when I set up Malik to get robbed by Kolyon, to getting set up by Lil Mexico with the department shit. My life was going outta control right in front of me and my dumbass couldn't even see it.

I sat up in my bed and stared at my dresser, looking at photos of my children in picture frames, when my eyes caught a pink book hiding under some booking reports. I grabbed it, it read, Holy Bible, two simple words. I stared at the cover, gently placing my hand over the title, I felt a sense of guilt over me, knowing damn well I had not been making choices God would be happy with. I didn't want to feel like a hypocrite, running to God when times are bad, but damn who could I turn to at a time like this. My mama was stressed as it was and my homegirls were busy dealing with the streets. Anika continuously checked on me; I just didn't wannabe bothered. Before I knew it, I had opened the bible and started to read, "Psalms, 41," this was the ending to all the bullshit in my life. I began feeling like I had a second chance to redeem my soul and restore a new way of life. Now I know the shit sounds cliché as hell, but I swear I felt a weight lifted off me. During my court proceedings and the bail bond ethics committee meetings, I didn't stress. I let go and let God. I was becoming more appreciative of the things in front of me, my children and how they laughed, I became more in tune to others around me and most of all the urge to live a stable, healthier, a more spiritual environment. Six months after joining Mt. Hermon Christian Ministries, I decided to give my life to the Lord and was baptized, my mom, children and Anika were all present, an experience I'd never forget.

The case was still active, a lot of motions, rescheduled court dates and people going unserved for court appearances. The case that was expected to last a maximum of ninety days, turned out to be a lot longer. This affected my finances in a major way; the bail bond ethics committee refused to reinstate my license from the prior suspension all because I had a pending 'act of violence' charge. Although my bank accounts were almost depleted, and Malik refused to help me financially even with the kids, and refused to communicate with any of one us, I knew my faith was being tested. Things had never been this bad before. But they say God gives his toughest battles to those who empower strength and will and I sometimes had to remind myself of that! It had been 270 days since the day I was charged with Aggravated Battery and finally I got a break, ole homegirl had a sudden change of heart and wrote an affidavit stating she didn't want to pursue charges and she would like for the charges to be dropped. My lawyer called me into his office to share the good news, "Well Asia, looks like the state's case against you is weakening, the victim wrote an affidavit asking for the charges to be dismissed," he grinned widely as he handed me over a copy of the affidavit.

As I read the eight-sentence statement, my eyes began to water with emotion, "I can't believe this. I swear God is really working," I said softly, still in disbelief, yet grateful and thankful.

"Hopefully the state will reconsider going to trial. I'll reach out to them first thing Monday morning, Asia," Zac stated, "I'll call you as soon as I hear something," he added as I stood up and headed towards his door, affidavit in hand, excited to meet with the committee regarding my case and request again for my license to be reinstated.

When Monday arrived Zac called with less enthusiasm in his voice, "Asia the state is playing hard ball and refusing to drop the charge right now."

Although that wasn't what I expected, I responded joyfully, "Zac it's ok and everything will be ok. I just left my ethics meeting and the bail bond committee has decided to reinstate my license, based on her affidavit, so if they don't decide to drop them right away, it's ok now." I hung up the phone, I was so feeling entirely blessed that the news about the state didn't even phase me. God answered one of my prayers. I was given back my license, ready to gain back clients, ready to reinvent the office and the company's name, a fresh start.

So your girl was back on her grind heavy, hired some more staff, keeping my office open literally twenty-four hours. I even hired an additional agent to keep the clock going and the bonds posted. Six weeks after being on straight grind mode, I decided to open another office in a neighboring county about an hour away, expanding the name. Things were beginning to look up, even the communication started to reestablish between Malik and I. He even started to see the kids again, but don't think your girl went soft, I just learned to let things go allowing myself to be more at peace, but believe me I didn't trust the nigga for shit. It was like he was, and might still be, sleeping with the enemy. I didn't care that she had written that statement, all of my guards were still all up.
"Damn baby mama, how you holding up and what's going on with your case?" He asked as though concerned.
"Well I figured you'd know more than me, but I'm good just maintaining, getting things back in order." I replied, playing chess not checkers. I knew my baby daddy couldn't be trusted. Although at times there were awkward silences between us I tried to make the best of it for the kids, but my baby daddy was a snake. Yeah I know I'm one too, but have you ever seen two snakes side by side, hanging out? Didn't think so and that's how I knew Malik and I could never be back together. Although he continued to shoot his shot towards us being a family, even taking me on a few trips to other states here and there, my heart would not allow me to give in and eventually he got over it, still a little spiteful but he was manageable to deal with.
Anika has and will forever be the sister I never had. She rode with me through some of my toughest battles and never allowed the streets to taint her with the bullshit, like it did with Meme and a few other fake friends. She finally opened up her shop and we both bossed up on our entrepreneurship, her and I were real sisters, fuck what DNA said, she was my dawg, my rider, and my big sister.

Rico confused ass still tried to keep communication open between us randomly posting subliminal quotes and shit on his IG story and even texted me from time to time. Crazy as this sounds that negro kept telling me I had the best pussy ever and that he could convert over only to a woman if I'd take him back. *Yeah right.* But crazy as the shit may sound he had been a great person to vent to, he had a real listening ear, go figure he'd be into guys.

Lil Mexico learned that you don't bite the hand that feeds you. A shit load of forfeitures, in debt with her insurance company, shit wasn't booming and before I knew it, she closed her office doors and turned in her license cause she was too broke and couldn't pay back the few bonds she did write. Greed is a real disease.

As for me, my kids were growing up and started to show their unique and adorable personalities while giving me their silent encouragement to keep moving forward in a positive direction. My mom started to live her own life as well, hanging out with friends, going on dates and low-key streaming on Tender. I'm just glad she got her groove back and reduced her stress about me and my on-going legal situation. *Yep who would of thought this bullshit was still going,* hell I don't know at this point if it's the state attorney's office moving like some damn turtles or if my attorney friend isn't really going to war for me. While clients of mine go to jail two to three times a year for battery and get their cases dropped within ninety days, my case was almost a whole year in. They say good things happen to those who wait, but how much waiting did I really have to do and why does Zachary keep rescheduling court appearances? Only time will tell, until then I will continue to grow in my faith and move in a positive less crowd-pleasing way. Throughout all of this chaos I learned two things: watch the company you keep because only those close to you can hurt you, and like Biggie said, more money, more problems.

BAIL MONEY

ABOUT THE AUTHOR

Born in the Florida Keys, raised by her hard-working mother who was diagnosed with cancer. Raised in a trailer park, with no siblings, Tia's always had to fend for herself. A graduate of Hodges University she holds a degree in Criminal Justice. Tia became a mother at the age of 22, deciding to make a career change, she became a bail bond agent. In 2012 she opened her bail bond company right before giving birth to her second child.

Subjected to several violent vandalism incidents and threatening phone calls she never gave up, opening a second location in 2018. Tia learned that the same rules applied in the streets are applied in the business world too.

"I thank the Lord continuously for blessing me with the drive, ambition and courage, and for never allowing a negative situation to determine my fate."

Tia Hanna

www.ingramcontent.com/pod-product-compliance
Lightning Source LLC
LaVergne TN
LVHW041458070426
835507LV00009B/667